Food in China

Polly Goodman

PowerKiDS
press.

New York

Published in 2008 by The Rosen Publishing Group, Inc.
29 East 21st Street, New York, NY 10010

First Edition

Editor: Sarah Gay
Senior Design Manager: Rosamund Saunders
Designer: Tim Mayer
Consultant: Susannah Blake

Library of Congress Cataloging-in-Publication Data

Goodman, Polly.
    Food in China / Polly Goodman. — 1st ed.
        p. cm. — (Food around the world)
    Includes index.
    ISBN 978-1-4042-4297-5 (library binding)
    1. Cookery, Chinese—Juvenile literature. 2. Food
habits—China—Juvenile literature. I. Title.
    TX724.5.C5G575 2008
    641.5951—dc22

                                          2007032607

Manufactured in China

Cover photograph: street vendors at a colorful
market in Beijing.

Photo credits: Jose Fuste Raga/Corbis 6, Nevada
Wier/CORBIS 8, Wayland Picture Library 9, 16 and 17,
Andrew Sydenham/Anthony Blake Photo Library 10,
Keren Su/Lonely Planet 11, Martin Brigdale/Anthony
Blake Photo Library 12, China Photos/Reuters/Corbis 13
and title page, Yann Layma/Getty Images 14, Tim
Hill/Anthony Blake Photo Library 15, Ips Co
Ltd/Photolibrary 18, Mark Henley/Panos Pictures 19,
Greg Elms/LonelyPlanet 20, Ric Ergenbright/CORBIS 21,
Richard Jones/sinopix 22, Royalty-Free/Corbis 23,
Rawdon Wyatt/Anthony Blake Photo Library 24, Oliver
Strewe/Lonely Planet 25, Eaglemoss Consumer
Publications/Anthony Blake Photo Library 26, Jon
Hicks/CORBIS cover.

Contents

Welcome to China   6

Farming and weather   8

Rice and wheat   10

Vegetables, pulses, and fruit   12

Fish and meat   14

Shopping and street food   16

Mealtimes in China   18

Around the country   20

Special occasions   22

Festival food   24

Make some Chinese soup!   26

A balanced diet   27

Glossary   28

Further information and Web Sites   29

Index   30

Words in **bold** can be found in the glossary on page 28

Welcome to China

China is the largest country in Asia. People have been cooking delicious dishes there since ancient times. Today, Chinese tea, rice, and noodle dishes are popular all over the world. There are hundreds of different dishes, cooked in various ways.

▼ *China has mountains, valleys, deserts, **plains**, rivers, and islands.*

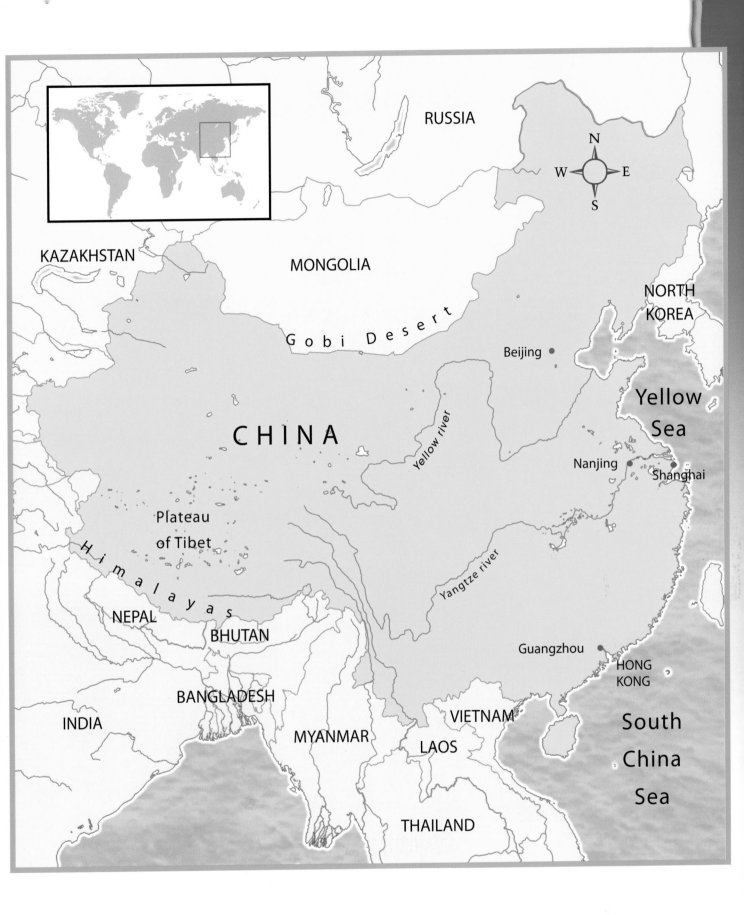

RUSSIA

KAZAKHSTAN

MONGOLIA

NORTH KOREA

G o b i   D e s e r t

Beijing

Yellow Sea

CHINA

Yellow river

Nanjing

Shanghai

Plateau of Tibet

H i m a l a y a s

Yangtze river

NEPAL

BHUTAN

Guangzhou

HONG KONG

BANGLADESH

South China Sea

INDIA

VIETNAM

MYANMAR

LAOS

THAILAND

▲ *China is marked in orange on this map. It has more people than any other country in the world.*

Farming and weather

China stretches from the high Himalayan mountains in the west, to the **fertile** valleys of the Yellow and Yangtze rivers in the east. Some foods grow well in Southern China where it is hot and wet. Other foods grow well in the north where it is very dry.

▼ Women herd sheep in the dry mountains of Northwest China.

The hot, **humid** south is ideal for growing rice. Farmers also raise pigs, chickens, and ducks. In the north and west, it is too dry to grow rice, so wheat and corn are grown instead. Sheep and cows graze in the hills.

▲ *Farmers use buffalo to pull plows through the wet rice fields.*

Rice and wheat

Rice is eaten with most meals in Southern China. It is boiled and often fried with meat, seafood, eggs, or vegetables. Rice is sometimes boiled in beef or vegetable stock to make a souplike dish called **congee**.

▼ Rice was boiled, then fried with eggs and peas to make this dish of egg-fried rice.

Wheat flour is used to make noodles, pancakes, steamed buns, and dumplings. Noodles are **stir-fried** or added to soups. Pancakes and dumplings are steamed and filled with meat or vegetables.

▲ When fresh noodles are made, they are hung out in the sun to dry.

Food fact
Chinese noodles can be made from wheat, rice, soybeans, eggs, or corn.

Vegetables, pulses, and fruit

Vegetables are very important in Chinese cooking. Beansprouts, bamboo shoots, water chestnuts, and mushrooms are all popular. **Pulses** are also used in many Chinese dishes. Soybeans are used to make **soy sauce** and **bean curd**.

▼ *This dish is a mixture of fried bean curd and Chinese shiitake mushrooms.*

Tropical fruits such as mango, **lychees**, **starfruit**, kiwifruit, bananas, and **papaw** are grown in China. People eat them fresh and use them to make desserts and drinks.

▲ Some Chinese towns hold lychee festivals. Everybody tastes the ripe lychee fruits.

Fish and meat

China has over 1,200 miles (2,000 kilometers) of coastline where prawns, lobster, **shad**, and mullet are caught. Prawns are also kept in ponds on fish farms. Perch and other freshwater fish are caught in China's rivers. Fish is usually steamed or stir-fried.

▼ *Fishermen sort a large catch of fish into baskets.*

◀ Crispy fried duck, spring onions, and cucumber are rolled in steamed pancakes. This dish is called Peking Duck.

Pork is the most common meat in China. Chicken and duck are also popular. They are cooked slowly in stews, stir-fried, or steamed.

Food fact

Chickens are kept for their eggs, which are used in many Chinese dishes.

Shopping and street food

Fresh fruit, vegetables, meat, and fish are sold in open markets. There are also small general stores selling rice, milk, and other everyday goods. Some big towns and cities have large supermarkets.

◄ There is an open market in every Chinese village, town, and city.

On city streets, people sell traditional Chinese food, such as steamed buns and watermelon seeds, or pork and cabbage rolls called **chiaotse**. They make quick snacks or lunches for office workers.

◀ Steamed buns filled with meat and vegetables are made by a street vendor.

Food fact
The Chinese love jasmine tea and green tea, which are drunk without milk or sugar.

Mealtimes in China

Everyday Chinese meals might include dishes from the menus below.

Breakfast

Rice porridge with dumplings

Doughnut with hot **soymilk**

Milk or jasmine tea

Lunch

Vegetable noodle soup

Chinese leaves with bean curd

◀ *The Chinese drink jasmine or green tea with most meals.*

Dinner

Peanut salad

Radish and carrot pickle

Red-braised pork with chestnuts

Steamed fish in lotus leaves

Stir-fried cauliflower

Red-braised mushrooms

Vegetable soup

Fresh watermelon

Fresh oranges

Jasmine or green tea

▲ *The Chinese eat with chopsticks, which they hold between their thumb and their first two fingers.*

Around the country

Each region of China has its own special style of cooking. In the south, rice is the most important food and **dimsum** are often eaten. Pork is the most common type of meat in the south. In the east, people eat fish, clear soups, and **jiaozi** dumplings.

◄ Dimsum are steamed or fried snacks, such as spring rolls, prawn dumplings, or pork buns.

In Western China, hot and spicy dishes are made with **Sichuan peppercorns** and chilies. In the north, wheat noodles are more common than rice. Peking duck, fried bean curd, and **water chestnuts** are favorites in this region.

▲ Noodles are often served in a soup, such as this bowl of vegetable and noodle soup.

Special occasions

On birthdays, weddings, and other special occasions, people eat foods that have special meanings. Noodles are eaten at birthday parties, because they stand for a long and happy life.

◀ These birthday buns have been made to look like peaches. In China, peaches stand for a long life.

Food fact

In China, foods have different meanings. Sugar stands for a sweet life and oranges mean wealth.

Chinese weddings can last for up to four days, and the highlight of each day is a feast. Red dishes are often served because red is the color of happiness. By eating these dishes, the guests wish the bride and groom a happy marriage.

▲ Chinese wedding cakes are baked and filled with red or green bean paste.

Festival food

The biggest festival in China is the New Year Festival. In Northern China, families put a coin inside one of their jiaozi dumplings. Whoever finds it is wished good luck for the new year. In the south, people eat a special sticky cake, which stands for friendships lasting.

◀ *Vegetable spring rolls look like gold bars and represent wealth in the new year.*

The Moon Festival takes place on the day of the new moon, in September or October each year. Families get together and eat round cakes with sweet centers, called moon cakes.

▼ A tray of freshly baked moon cakes is ready for the Moon Festival.

Make some Chinese soup!

What you need

1 can of corn

2 spring onions

3 cups (750ml) chicken stock

1 cup (170g) cooked chicken, diced

1 tablespoon sugar

What to do

1. Slice the spring onions finely.
2. Put the corn and spring onions in a saucepan with the chicken and stock.
3. Boil and simmer with a lid on for 10 minutes.
4. Add the sugar and simmer for 5 minutes.

Ask an adult to help you make this soup. Always be careful with sharp knives and hot pans.

Food pyramid

This food pyramid shows which foods you should eat to have a healthy, **balanced diet**.

We shouldn't eat too many fats, oils, cakes, and candies.

Milk, cheese, meat, fish, beans, and eggs help to keep us strong.

We should eat plenty of vegetables and fruit to keep healthy.

Bread, cereal, rice, and pasta should make up most of our diet.

Chinese meals use all foods from the pyramid. Some dishes are fried in oil, but most are made of rice or noodles with vegetables and some fish or meat, which helps to balance Chinese diets.

Glossary

balanced diet   a diet that includes a mixture of different foods, which supplies all the things a body needs to keep healthy

bean curd   a paste made from mashed soybeans

chiaotse   rolls of pastry filled with pork and cabbage

congee   a souplike dish made from rice boiled in beef or vegetable stock

dimsum   steamed or fried snacks, such as spring rolls, prawn dumplings, or pork buns

fertile   land that is good for growing crops

humid   moist or damp

jiaozi   dumplings filled with pork mince and Chinese cabbage or other fillings

lychee   a sweet, fleshy fruit with a spiny skin

papaw   a fruit with an orange flesh and small black seeds

plain   a large area of flat land

pulses   beans, peas, and other foods that are edible seeds

shad   a type of fish in the herring family

Sichuan peppercorns   the dried seeds of a plant grown in the Sichuan province of China, which give food a hot taste

soymilk   a rich, creamy milk made from soybeans

soy sauce   a sauce made from soybeans

starfruit   a yellow, star-shaped fruit with a ribbed skin

stir-fried   a dish that has been fried rapidly while stirring and tossing

water chestnuts   the edible roots of a plant that grows in freshwater ponds, marshes, and lakes

Further information

Books to read

A World of Recipes: China by Julie McCulloch (Heinemann, 2001)

Country Insights: China by Julia Waterlow (Raintree, 1997)

Kids Around the World Celebrate!: The Best Feasts and Festivals from Many Lands by Lynda Jones (Jossey-Bass, 1999)

Let's Eat! What Children Eat Around the World by Beatrice Hollyer (Henry Holt and Co, 2004)

Moonbeams, Dumplings, and Dragon Boats: A Treasury of Chinese Holiday Tales, Activities and Recipes by Nina Simonds and Leslie Swartz (Gulliver Books, 2002)

We Come From China by Julia Waterlow (Raintree, 1999)

Web Sites
Due to the changing nature of Internet links, PowerKids Press has developed an online list of Web sites related to the subject of this book. This site is regularly updated. Please use this link to access this list: www.powerkidslinks.com/faw/china

Index

All the numbers in **bold** refer to photographs as well as text.

A

animals   8–9, **8–9**, 15

B

birthdays   22
breakfast   18

C

corn   9

D

desserts   13, 24–25, **25**
dinner   19
drinks   6, 13, 17, 18, **18**, 19
dumplings   11, 20, **20**, 24

F

fruit   13, **13**, 16, 17, 22

L

lunch   17, 18

M

market   16, **16**
meat   10, 15, **15**, 16, 17, 19, 20, 21
Moon Festival 25

N

New Year   24
noodles   6, 11, **11**, 18, 21, **21**, 22

P

pulses   12, **12**, 21

R

rice   6, 9, **9**, 10, **10**, 16, 18, 20, 21

S

seafood   10, 14, **14**, 16
spices   21
street food   17, **17**
shops   16

T

tea   6, 17, 18, **18**, 19

V

vegetables   10, 12, **12**, 16, 17, 18, 19, 21, **21**, 24, **24**

W

weather   8–9
weddings   22–23
wheat   9, 11